T0068143

THE LORD'S BLESSING

In His Own Words

ALBERT LAWRENCE

WESTBOW
PRESS®
A DIVISION OF THOMAS NELSON
& ZONDERVAN

WestBow Press books may be ordered through booksellers or by contacting:

WestBow Press
A Division of Thomas Nelson & Zondervan
1663 Liberty Drive
Bloomington, IN 47403
www.westbowpress.com
844-714-3454

All Scripture quotations are taken from the Holy Bible, New International Version®, NIV®. Copyright ©1973, 1978, 1984, 2011 by Biblica, Inc.® Used by permission of Zondervan. All rights reserved worldwide. www.zondervan. com The "NIV" and "New International Version" are trademarks registered in the United States Patent and Trademark Office by Biblica, Inc.®

ISBN: 978-1-6642-5522-7 (sc)
ISBN: 978-1-6642-5523-4 (e)

Print information available on the last page.

WestBow Press rev. date: 03/17/2022

Contents

Contents

Acknowledgements

I wish to dedicate this book to several clergy whom God used to lead me into the career in ordained ministry. These two clergy served in a Lutheran Church in suburban Washington, D.C. congregation during my college years at the University of Maryland. The Rev. Bob Logan, currently retired, together with The Rev. E. Raymond Shaheen, now deceased, gave me their insights and counsel relating to all aspects of ordained ministry. More than five decades of serving in four congregations in four states have shown the wisdom of the decision.

I also want to give my sincere thanks to Mrs. Barbara Spell, a Westbow author in her own right, for her helpful corrections and suggestions as she read and commented on the manuscript several times.

My prayer for you, the reader, is that this book will deepen your appreciation and understanding of God's timeless blessing and allow you to receive it again and again.

Introduction

The Tiny Window into The Past

Archaeologists have got to be some of the most patient and persevering people in the world. They are not treasure hunters but seekers of anything that would give them a window into past cultures. They are respectable scientists in how they are looking for evidence of what it was like to live in those ancient days. As they dig not only with a shovel but also with a teaspoon, their eyes are trained to spot clues that might lead to other clues and facts about the past.

In the city of Jerusalem, in Israel "David's City," is a small section of land going south from the Temple area. There you will find several tombs which were surprisingly untouched by centuries, even millennia of previous generations of God's people.

On that hot, cloudless day in July 1969, Dr. Gabriel Barkay and his team were examining a burial site and a few empty tombs long ago plundered of any interesting artifacts. Usually that meant arrowheads, ivory pieces of jewelry, and pottery pieces. On this day he was working with his team of assistants and helpers, some of the volunteers being teenagers.

He uncovered the remains of a Byzantine church with a mosaic floor and a few tombs cut out of the rock with roofs that had collapsed. Looking carefully, he saw that the tombs had already been robbed of anything valuable. Among the team members there was a 13-year-old boy named Nathan who had been sent off to clean one of the tombs from the rubble. Dr. Barkay told young Nathan to clean the area because the photographer was going to come and take pictures.

After Nathan was finished cleaning, he got bored and started to bang randomly with his hammer on the rocks. To his great surprise the stone floor gave way and revealed that he had broken into the ceiling of another tomb below. He went back and told Dr. Barkay. The two were joined by a whole team of people, and together they found two feet of accumulated artifacts: There were semi-precious stones, arrowheads, ivory, glass, gold and silver. Then came the discovery of an ancient pendant or amulet containing some rolled up silver scrolls.

Unrolled, one amulet is nearly four inches long and the other is an inch and a half long and about a half inch wide. On the smaller one there is more detail in addition to the famous blessing. It reads. "May he/she be blessed by YHWH, the warrior /helper and the rebuker of evil." "YHWH keeps the covenant and graciousness towards those who love (him) and keep (his commandments)....for YHWH is our restorer and rock." Then follows the blessing we are studying. YHWH are the four letters which abbreviate the Hebrew word for Yahweh, which stands for Jehovah, the name of Almighty God.

Obviously, these scrolls were not intended for reading. The letters are far too small, and the writing is concealed inside the scrolls. There are about 100 words arranged in 12 lines of text. The person who did the writing was able to fit all of that onto a silver sheet the length of a matchstick!

This begs the question: If these tiny inscriptions were not meant for reading, what purpose did they have? They were designed to create a sense of intimacy between the god or goddess and the wearer. As they dangled comfortably from the neck, the wearer had the feeling that their god was close to the heart. It was easy enough for Hebrews to adapt that same idea to amulets of their own making and to texts from the Bible. The words would come to mind constantly. The Psalmist put it this way:

> "I have hidden your word in my heart that I might not sin
> against you." (Psalm 119:11)

In the ancient world amulets were taken seriously. Similar language is found in the Dead Sea Scrolls, the most famous of archaeological discoveries some 400 years later. Having this kind of reminder of demons and evil powers caused believers to remember God's promise to be present with them for protection.

The next step was to unroll the scrolls without serious damage. After much consultation the archeologists began their careful work. When finished, they were excited to be able to read the ancient Hebrew script with the letters YHWH, the four-letter name of God, clearly etched into the silver.

We wonder who the woman was who wore this pendant. The pagan cultures around the Jews had their amulets with the name of the god(s) engraved. Wearing the amulet as a kind of pendant was for protection against evil, calamity or bodily harm. In the same manner, while this woman was copying the words of the Lord's blessing, she was reminding herself to trust in the real God of the Bible for her protection and guidance.

Christians wear the cross for much the same reason. The cross identifies us as followers of Jesus Christ. For some, however, it is no more than wearing a college ring. It identifies them as Christians but to such people themselves it is often no more than a piece of jewelry.

Have you ever seen someone wearing a replica of a gallows or gas chamber on a chain? Neither have I. The cross could be no more than a symbol of death, but ironically, the fact is that it is really a symbol of life.

Only you know what the cross means to you. These days it is taking courage in some places to be wearing one. It should be something like the American flag. The flag should remind you of the words of the national anthem, and the story behind the brave Americans standing up to the powerful British military in 1812. It should mean that you are grateful for the privileges of being a citizen of this great country. If we can be proud to be an American, who pledges allegiance to the flag and the republic for which it stands, we can proudly pledge allegiance to the cross and the God for whom it stands.

It is the cross which reminds us that Jesus Christ takes our place, gives us his righteousness in exchange for our sins, his perfect obedience in exchange for our disobedience. Such a trade is for every believer to make. With that reassurance comes the kind of spiritual security we need and which only Christ our Savior can give.

I have not written this book from being fascinated about the discovery of a piece of jewelry from the early part of the seventh century, B.C. Nor have I written it to call attention to the fact that this discovery is evidence of the friendship between science and religion. They are not opposed to each other any more than spelling is opposed to arithmetic. They are simply two different venues to different kinds of truth.

What I want you to take from this book is an inner assurance that God always has the last word. He is always in control. He has always kept His promises. The Savior He sent is always the same, yesterday today and forever. Perfection does not need updating or upgrading.

"I am the Lord I do not change." (Malachi 3:6).

Remember that the three lines of the ancient blessing did not originate with Moses or Aaron or Joshua or any other human being in the Biblical account. These lines are quite literally the very words of God, dictated by God Himself! They were originally pronounced and declared by the high priest over the great crowd of God's people who had been slaves in Egypt. Their long trek to the promised land of freedom had just begun. It would be a very long and slow journey with many problems along the way. But God was clearing the path before them, and removing the resistance they encounted as they moved slowly forward. Each night the high priest would pronounce the Lord's blessing we read in Numbers 6. God never revised the blessing. That means that this blessing is also for us to read and believe. We need His protection, His grace and His peace for our life's journey as much as the ancient Hebrews. The good news is that the blessing always remains fresh, always relevant, and without any need of updating for every different time in history.

Chapter 1

The Favor of God

The Lord bless you" (Numbers 6:22)

When I think about the miraculous rescue operation in the days of Moses, I like to remember the time when my wife and I crossed the mighty Mississippi river on foot. We had no need of God's help and no need for a miracle.

Here is how it happened. Dawn and I were living in Minnesota at the time. On one summer vacation we were exploring the northern lake district and the area around Lake Itasca. The state of Minnesota calls itself the state with a thousand lakes.

The Mississippi river is 50 feet deep and 2,300 ft wide at the capital city of Baton Rouge, Louisiana. But at Lake Itasca, Minnesota it is only two feet deep and 20 feet wide. Large stones in the water beckon the tourist to jump from stone to stone and then be qualified to go home and tell friends that they walked across the Mississippi!

Walking across the Red Sea was a different story. It is 18 miles wide at the narrowest point and more than 150 feet deep. God's people did need a miracle to make a dramatic exit from Egypt. God led the greatest rescue operation ever.

No doubt many of you recall the blockbuster movie, "Ten Commandments," starring Charlton Heston as Moses. It was a masterpiece of cinema photography. I remember the incredible cleavage of the Red Sea waters, a wall of water on each side, people walking on dry land

1

while chariots from Egypt were hurrying to catch up to them and bring them back.

Watching the gripping drama, I imagined how the actual event happened. It was hard to realize just how much people suffered during those long years of captivity in Egypt. It was the time when human dignity was stolen from people whose value was simply to produce bricks for Pharaoh. They must have wondered if God had deserted them. Little did they know of the enormous rescue operation which God had in mind.

However, as we read the history of those times, it seems as though it was easier for God to get them out of Egypt than it was to get Egypt out of them. On the other side of the Red Sea they were stalled. They lacked the strong direction of Moses, their leader who was absent while getting direction from God on the mountain nearby. The crowds camping out at the foot of the mountain grew impatient.

If ever they needed strong leadership, it was right then. Aaron, the brother of Moses tried, but the people did not listen to his words. This did not bode well for them, as their lapse into idolatry would show. What they needed was this blessing from God to reassure them that He had not deserted them.

In mid-2022 many people have also wondered the same thing. It was because of the worldwide epidemic which began in 2020. The number of new cases of the Corona virus known as Covid 19 continues to put fear in the hearts of people everywhere. Whoever would have imagined that the whole world would so rapidly be under attack by this silent and invisible enemy? Where was God? Had He allowed this virus to be the curse that brought human beings to know the reality of a deadly infectious disease? We need to believe that God is still in control of our world. We need His blessing to remind us that nothing escapes His notice and His care.

The good news is that the blessing He gave to His people to encourage them as they began their journey to the land of promise has not expired. What He said in the days of Moses and the rescue of His people from oppression in Egypt still stands. It is not in need of updating or amending. No virus epidemic is about to gain the victory over Him. We trust in Him for whatever happens, and we believe that He is working in all things for our good and His glory.

As Moses and Joshua were receiving the Ten Commandments from

God, they also received this brief blessing of three lines of poetry. Each line is longer than the one before. There are six verbs which show us various aspects of God's character. There are no conditions attached. Obedience to His laws was not a condition of salvation for His people. God had already saved them. He did not make them clean up their acts before rescuing them and leading them miraculously on foot across the Red Sea. This illustrates that in the early stages of Old Testament history, God showed that He always acts from His undeserved grace and favor.

Many churches today use the words of this blessing as the parting benediction after worship has ended. The words are taken directly from the priestly blessing found in the book of Numbers, chapter 6.

"The Lord bless you and keep you. The Lord make his face shine upon you and be gracious unto you. The Lord turn his face toward you and give you peace." (Numbers 6:6-26)

"The Lord Bless You"

We begin our study of the blessing of the Lord by noticing that the Hebrew word "you" is singular. This enables the hearer to take it personally.

No one can borrow faith from someone else, and no one can do anyone's believing for them. "Group think" is a phenomenon of modern American culture where people like to echo each other's beliefs. God, however, respects the thoughts of the individual. With God, it is always personal and individual. Faith is never a borrowed thing.

Each of these lines in the priestly blessing begins the same way: First, there is a word to identify who is doing the blessing, namely God Himself, Jehovah, Yahweh, the Almighty, Maker of heaven and earth. The first-person pronoun I is repeated. This emphasis is meant to remind the people that the Lord God Himself is speaking to individuals, not groups. At verse 27, the personal subject of the verb is repeated, as a way of making sure the identity of the speaker is not confused. It is not Moses, not Aaron, but God Himself who is dictating this blessing in His own words and with all His divine authority.

There are two "bookends" to the blessing here.

"The Lord spoke to Moses, saying "Speak to Aaron and
his sons, saying, thus you shall bless the people of Israel."
(Numbers 6:22)

After the blessing comes a comment from God about what He has
done.

"So shall they put my name on the people of Israel and I
will bless them." (Numbers 6:27)

In effect, God is saying that He is directing His followers to be
channels of His blessing. To Abraham He had declared many years before:

"I will bless those who bless you." (Genesis 12:3)

Abraham and his descendants were privileged to live under the favor
of God with real intention and purpose. To live life as it was designed
by God was truly a special blessing. The hope was that others would be
impressed and want to know more about Abraham's God so as to receive
the blessing themselves.

How clearly this foreshadows the future coming of the Lord Jesus
Christ. God did not intend for the Old Testament to become something
archaic which needed replacement. It is part one in the narrative which is
followed by and completed in part two, the gospel good news about the
coming of Yeshua, Messiah, Jesus of Nazareth. There is one unfolding
narrative all through the Bible, with two major divisions, the Old and
New Testaments (Covenants).

Does God withhold His blessing until we deserve it?

God does not withhold His blessing on His people until first they
"clean up their act." When God heard their cry from oppression under
Pharaoh, they did not yet have the law, the Ten Commandments. First
came the rescue, and then the law. They did not earn or deserve the rescue,
they were rescued because God is a God of mercy and compassion, and
He remembered His Covenant. The motive for the people to obey the
commandments was duty, not to cause God to act, but to say thank you
for what He had already done. There was no "quid pro quo." Earning and
deserving never entered His mind.

But I wonder if you noticed that God did not "fire" Aaron for leading a rebellion. Eventually God questioned him about this blatant idolatry. It was some ancient version of "What were you thinking?"

Never mind that Aaron was the brother of Moses. Aaron led a full-scale rebellion against the God who had saved their lives. Yes, for a minute God's anger burned against Aaron's inexcusable actions. God considered destroying the whole crowd. However, He had promised Noah that such action would never happen again. Aaron had no defense for his idolatry and offered the flimsiest of excuses to God. In effect, Aaron was saying that he had lost control and did not even try to regain it. What has always puzzled me is how easily Aaron allowed the idolatry and even supported it.

Moses then interceded and sought God's forgiveness.

> "Do not bring disaster upon your people; remember Abraham, Isaac and Jacob to whom you swore to give the Promised Land as an inheritance." (Deuteronomy 4:38)

The people were still His people. They were still sinners, but still heirs of His promise.

God heard Moses' prayer and then reconsidered.

Perhaps this was an advance peek into the future and to the gospel of Christ. Fast forward to the time of Christ many centuries later to about 33 A.D. See the gruesome place where Jesus was being crucified just outside Jerusalem. Two criminals, one on either side of Jesus, were also dying by this cruel method. They were suffering from murder and what we would call terrorist activity. The death penalty of crucifixion means that they were considered to be the worst of criminals. One of them, however, was sorry for what he had done.

Jesus, just a few feet away, could read this man's mind. Though he was guilty, he was also sincerely penitent. He said to Jesus:

> "Jesus, remember me when you come into your kingdom."
> Jesus answered him, "I tell you the truth, today you will be with me in paradise." (Luke 23:42,43)

Jesus could have said nothing. Certainly he did not need to speak at all. But he saw it as an opportunity to apply the gospel truth he was born to give to all people. He wanted to express that love just one more time before he died. The penitent criminal provided the perfect example of undeserved grace. All his life Jesus illustrated this great gospel truth: *There is nothing that we can do to make God love us more, and there is nothing that we can do to make Him love us less.*

This is not to cheapen or take God's forgiveness for granted. We are always required to confess our sin and ask in faith to be forgiven. That is not presumption but preparation to receive God's undeserved grace. However, the law of God does not come first, but after grace. Rescue does not come with conditions that must first be met. Remember that God led His people out of Egypt and across the Red Sea on dry land before anyone had ever seen or heard of the Ten Commandments!

We need to define the word blessing as the Bible meant us to understand it. When we look back to the original Hebrew meaning in context, we find that it simply means receiving something of value as an expression of favor or affection from God. It is not a prize or reward but rather a kind of inheritance.

No conditions are attached to a blessing; it is simply the work of God in the community of faith. Therefore, these words of God through Aaron were to be pronounced, declared, invoked every day upon the people of God on their journey to the promised land.

"The Lord bless you...."

This is the first line of a three-line benediction heard at the end of an evening worship service. The Hebrew word for 'bless' means to do or give something of value to another out of pure love. I picture my two-year-old grandson running down the long hallway of my house and into my open arms. I kneel to be on his level as I give him a bear hug.

In a similar way, God laid aside His divine prerogatives and glory to stoop down to become one of us. Yeshua, Messiah, was conceived supernaturally with two separate natures, human and divine. It was an expression of God's humbling of Himself. Paul wrote so eloquently in his letter to the Philippians:

"Christ Jesus, who being in very nature God, did not consider equality with God something to be grasped, but made himself nothing, taking the very nature of a servant, being made in human likeness. And being found in appearance as a man, he humbled himself and became obedient to death ...even death on a cross." (Philippians 2:6-12)

Blessing is an exercise in humility for both God and human beings. In some churches the posture of kneeling for prayer is designed to make us think of this two-sided expression of humility. He humbles Himself to give; we humble ourselves to receive. Think of a subject kneeling in front of a king. Think of a lover kneeling on one knee, asking his beloved for her hand in marriage.

God blessed them with His "shalom" which is wholeness, wellbeing and peace. That meant food, clothing, shelter, happiness in their family life, a good reputation in their community, good health, long life, protection from enemies, fruitful crops and leisure to rest. They dreamed for the time when they might live in a world with no suffering or pain but in the enjoyment of God's favor.

Just as important as having those good things was the knowledge of where the blessings came from. The Jews were not to think that they could bless themselves or achieve their blessings by some earning or deserving of their own. God wanted them to see their blessings as His gifts and not as reward or entitlement. The truth is that too much prosperity can be a dangerous thing.

In Proverbs we find these wise words:

"Give me neither poverty nor riches but give me only my daily bread. Otherwise, I may have too much and disown you and say, 'Who is the Lord? Or I may become poor and steal, and so dishonor the name of my God." (Proverbs 30:8,9)

A psychologist would take those verses and tell you that this is the root problem of living in a culture like America today. Daily bread is always getting redefined. Wants become needs as we get used to one level of abundance, and then desire more. That is called "the law of adaptation." It seems that we never learn to say "enough."

Interestingly, the word "you" is singular in each of the three ways God blesses. The idea is that anyone who hears it will make God his or her own Lord. It is as if God wants the people to remember Who is speaking this benediction. It is no less than the One from whom all blessings flow. We cannot emphasize too much the given quality of God's character. The character of God is what it is, and we must remember that we did not come up with it. It is therefore futile for us to amend, soften or omit any aspect of it. We cannot edit out or airbrush away what we don't like about what Scripture says.

"I the Lord do not change" (Malachi 3:6)

This truth is more obvious as we get to the second, or New Testament. In a brief note, one of the physical stepbrothers of Christ, was a man named Jude. He calls people to believe in the unvarnished truth about the gospel. Good news follows bad news. Then as now there were people who would take the hard sayings of Jesus and soften them to make them more attractive.

The answer then is the answer now. Do not try to remove the offense of the gospel. Let it be the background against which the truth of the gospel makes the mercy and grace of God so appealing and attractive.

Imagine yourself in a jewelry store looking at diamond engagement rings. The salesperson puts the diamond on a black velvet cushion so you can examine the color, size, brilliance and clarity of the gem. The black velvet enhances the beauty of the diamond.

Likewise, it is only when we hear the bad news of our sin against God that the good news of His grace becomes truly compelling and desirable.

That is why the gospel must not be softened and toned down. God did not send Jesus into the world to congratulate those who were making good moral "grades." Nor did He give us seven effective habits to take our own lives to the "next level" of satisfaction. No, He came into the world to save sinners. It comes by grace alone, through faith alone, and by Christ alone, but not by faith that is alone. True faith does lead to good deeds, but good deeds are always the fruit of such faith, not its cause.

Yes, the gospel is all grace from start to finish. In the Episcopal Church the Book of Common Prayer provides a General Confession to be said in unison: Sense as you read these words how difficult it is to be honest in what you are asked to say aloud. "We acknowledge and bewail our manifold sins and wickedness, which we from time to time most grievously have committed, provoking most justly thy wrath and indignation against us. We do earnestly repent and are heartily sorry for these our misdoings. The remembrance of them is grievous unto us, the burden of them is intolerable"[1]

Over the years people have told me that they do not feel honest in saying such words in prayer, and that the language is far too harsh. In 1979, a revision of the Prayer Book provided for a newer version of confession without the mention of God's wrath. I am not sure anyone is really the better for the change. It seems to be more geared to the change of the culture than to anything related to the forgiving nature of God.

The only explanation for the Prayer Book language being overly critical is not to confess to God the way we do feel about our sin, but the way we should feel, and the way God does feel. For many people the truth about sin has been softened and redefined simply because it seems more honest to do so.

The classic statement of how the culture blunts the sharpness of the Bible comes to us in Menninger's "Whatever Became of Sin?" book, published back in the 1970's. Briefly, his answer is that we have taken the guilt out of the word sin and renamed it a mistake, bad judgment, an illness, even a crime but nothing a quick apology won't fix. Over the past generation or two in our time there has been a coarsening of our culture. There has been a relaxation of the rules of what constitutes acceptable moral behavior.

When Jesus was teaching and preaching to the crowds he never minced words. He called a spade a spade. We read about one such incident when he had been speaking in the Capernaum synagogue. Jesus offended some people with his metaphor about eating flesh and drinking blood. Literally, it sounded like he was advocating cannibalism. What did he mean?

Jesus had said that he is the bread of life, and that unless we "eat" him, we will all die. Could this be a kind of veiled reference to the last supper Jesus would with his disciples? In the words of that highly symbolic metaphor, he would take bread and say:

> "This is my body which is for you, do this in remembrance of me." (1 Corinthians 11:24)

We must remember that in those days almost everybody worked on a farm and knew that food comes from plants, seafoods and animals. Were you to ask a child today where food comes from, he or she would answer that it comes from the grocery store.

Unlike our technological era, life in that agrarian society in Biblical times caused people to live close to nature and know firsthand about food sources. They knew that plants and animals and fish must die in order that we can have their life. It is what we mean by substitution. Something else dies, a vegetable, a fish, an animal, and we get to live. What is the hamburger? It is dead cow, lettuce, onion and tomato, all of which died to yield their life to us.

Carrying forward the metaphor, Jesus says,

> "unless you eat the flesh of the Son of Man and drink his blood you have no life in you." (John 6:52)

He is speaking figuratively, of course. But nonetheless, in a way beyond our comprehension, his life becomes ours as our death vicariously becomes his.

What he meant was that believing in him was to become as important to our souls as food and drink is important to our bodies. However, some people did not get the meaning of the metaphor. Instead they decided they had heard enough and no longer followed him. It was a classic example of how all of us have a tendency to want Jesus on our own terms or not at all. It can become a real hurdle to genuine faith.

Later on the apostle Paul wrote about the condition of being almost a Christian but not quite. It is the same as held true for his definition of a genuine Jew. In his letter to the Romans he writes:

> "A man is not a Jew if he is only one outwardly, nor is circumcision merely outward and physical. No, a man is a

> Jew if he is one inwardly; and circumcision is of the heart,
> by the spirit, not by the written code." (Romans 2:28,29)

Circumcision was the visible and outward sign of being a Jew. Substitute the word "Christian" for "Jew," and the meaning remains the same. Followers of Jesus must internalize what they believe. Otherwise, they remain in control of their lives and think of Christianity as just one more of many interests or hobbies. It is not whether or not we have Jesus Christ as we might have some cherished possession. No, it is whether or not Jesus Christ by His Spirit has us. When I see a man or woman wearing a shirt that says "property of the U.S. Government" I do not have to ask what that means. Likewise we accept that to follow Jesus is not something partial or part time, but completely and without reservation.

Chapter 2

The Care of God

"and keep you." (Numbers 6:24)

K ing David was a man with insight few others could match. David is the one most remembered by the metaphor of the shepherd. Many people down through the centuries have memorized the words of David in Psalm 23. I think his words in Psalm 16 are equally comforting. You will sometimes see them written on tombstones:

> "You have made known to me the path of life. You will
> fill me with joy in your presence, with eternal pleasures
> at your right hand."(Psalm 16:11)

In the Hebrew mind there was a positive note about dying as a believer. It was called being "gathered to one's fathers" or to "one's people." Sometimes death is softened into a process of "falling asleep."

It stands to reason, of course, that to be rewarded or punished requires a conscious form of existence in the hereafter. In the New Testament we read how Jesus made the same body/soul distinction but added the promise of everlasting life. For those whose sins are forgiven by the cross of Christ, dying becomes a transition to new and greater life. We die, but then again, we do not die. Only the body dies and returns to the ground. The soul lives on in eternal sorrow or joy.

A Jewish friend of mine now deceased resisted every attempt of mine to convince him of the truth of Christianity. I affirmed the need for all the Bible to be considered as one continuing narrative, and the first act in a long and extended two- part play. If that is true, it stands to reason that no one would want to come to see the first act of the play and then leave during intermission. By the same token, no Christian would want to come and see the play starting after the intermission and try to understand the plot starting with Act Two. The beginning is a good place to begin, not halfway through the play.

My friend could not see the simple logic. He was raised to believe that if Jesus really was the Messiah, God would not let Jesus fail. Messiah would never allow himself to suffer and die on the cross. That would be evidence enough that Christianity is not true. He also denied the resurrection and regarded it as a story made up by Jesus' followers. No, for him death would simply be the end of life, period. His body would be turned into fertilizer.

Nonetheless, he would watch a Christian television program where the preacher would always speak of Israel in a positive way. He, the preacher, would point out that the New Testament did not replace the Old Testament but carried forward God's continuing action in human history.

I like to think that perhaps in some quiet moment he kept secret, he did accept Yeshua, Jesus, as the long-awaited Messiah before he died. Only God knows.

Jude, the step- brother of Jesus

Another Bible benediction comes from the pen of one of the physical stepbrothers of Jesus, a man named Jude. At some point in his life, Jude became a real defender of the claims of Jesus. In a short letter from Jude, only one chapter in length, we have a strong defense of the true gospel.

Jude wrote to Christians to warn them about false teachers. These men had been teaching that Jesus was not the Son of God.

> "They are godless men, who change the grace of our God into a license for immorality," (Jude 4)

He ended his short letter with these timely words on the keeping role of God:

> "To him who is able to keep you from falling and to present you before his glorious presence without fault and with great joy…to the only God be glory, majesty, power and authority, through Jesus Christ our Lord, before all ages, now and forever more! Amen." (Jude 24)

The soul is the real you and the real me. It is the center of our being, our personality, mind, will and emotions. It is the non-material part of us, which cannot be measured. It has no mass, no weight, and is beyond any scientific analysis. It is beyond the reach of the laboratory.

The soul is the part of you that makes you the person you are.

Contrary to what most people think, death is not an ending but a beginning. Will it be endless sorrow or endless pleasure? Perishing means continued existence outside of heaven and being shut out from God's presence forever.

God sends nobody to such an existence; people volunteer for it. God respects the freedom He gave us and honors what we choose. If we have spent a lifetime wishing He would go away and leave us alone, He will grant our request, though it surely makes Him sad.

A personal experience concerning the soul comes to mind. It is difficult to define the soul, and more difficult to illustrate its meaning.

It was an ordinary day in a summer training program for clergy on how to minister to the sick back in 1963. The large teaching hospital in Minneapolis was the place where clergy like me listened to a lecture about what a hospital does. We were all dressed in white coats like the ones used by medical staff. We were standing outside the room where autopsies are performed. A hospital staff member lectured us about the procedure.

One of the orderlies standing near me whispered a question. "I see you are wearing a cross on your white coat. Are you a chaplain?"

"Yes," I replied, "We are all here on a training program for pastors called "Clinical Pastoral Education."

"Great," he said. "I have a question for you. I have seen a number of these post-mortem procedures, but I have never seen any of the doctors identify the soul. Could you tell me what part of the body contains the soul?"

The question was more profound than he realized. I did not have time to look up the official definition of the word "soul" in a theological dictionary, but I answered as best I could.

I asked, "Did you ever see that person before he died?"

"Oh, yes," he said. "I used to wheel him around back and forth from the third floor to the first."

I paused for a moment and then replied, "Well, perhaps I could put it this way. The difference between the person you saw alive up on the third floor and the body that is being analyzed for the cause of death is what we call the soul."

That was many years ago, but I would answer that question in the same way now. The young orderly's question reflected the assumptions of many people today. They wonder how body relates to soul.

The Greek philosophers Plato and Aristotle thought that the soul was in the prison house of the body and was released at the hour of death. Hence, they thought that it did not matter what a person did with the body, since it was totally separate from the soul, not just a compartment of it. The body was mortal, but the soul was immortal. The Greek word for soul is "psyche," from which we get the word psychology.

The Biblical view was different. In the Old Testament, we hear of people thinking with their hearts. This was not a reference to the physical organ which pumps blood. The heart was the seat of the emotions, the mind and the will. It is the control center of the personality. In Hebrew, soul referred to the whole being in a relationship with God and other people. It is like the computer's operating system, which connects all the different functions together and keeps them working in harmony.

Therefore, it is true that Christians die and yet they do not die. Keeping includes dying. Death is the doorway to more life. The body dies but the soul lives on. Like the Secret Service agent guarding the President, God watches your every move. He knows just what you are thinking and doing, even while you are sleeping.

> "He who watches over you will not slumber. Indeed, he
> who watches over Israel will neither slumber nor sleep."
> (Psalm 121:4)

Jesus illustrated God's watchful care in several powerful metaphors.

> "Are not two sparrows sold for a penny? Yet not one of them will fall to the ground apart from the will of your Father. So, do not be afraid; you are worth more than many sparrows." (Mathew 10:29)

The other metaphor is a short one.

> "Even the very hairs of your head are all numbered." (Matthew 10:30)

This is called hyperbole, which means exaggerating to make a point. It means that all our records are on file in the heavenly computers.

Did you ever wonder why God decided to take a certain group of people to call them His own and keep them in a relationship of trust and obedience to Him? He tells us in so many words. He says it was not because of anything they did to deserve it, but because of what he swore to their ancestors, Abraham, Isaac, and Jacob.

No, they were chosen because God chose them. Period. They were blessed because God entered a covenant with Abraham who became their founding father,

The interesting thing about the priestly prayer is that it was became the catalyst for supernatural things to happen during the travel to the land of promise.

God gave them special food to eat. It was a bread called "manna" which means "what is it?" I can almost hear in my mind many people asking for something the whole family will like. Maybe they were satisfied when God provided them with quail to eat as well as the manna. God knew their need and provided them with quail as their meat.

They also enjoyed the luxury of an ancient form of a global positioning system. It was a moving cloud by day and a moving fire by night. God was programming the direction and using the cloud and fire as their supernatural GPS. The evidence for His keeping watch over His people day and night was plain to see.

Keeping also conveys genuine acceptance as we are

We see this in our culture. Only the dates have changed. We human beings have always wanted love and approval by other people in in order to feel good about ourselves. We define our self-worth by just how much we feel accepted and approved by parents, siblings, friends, and associates at work. Face book "friends" also count.

It is tragic that so many people, especially men, feel that they must measure up to a standard of acceptance society sets for them. How easily we can become approval addicts. The problem behind our wanting approval so much is not the wanting but the source of the wanting. Approval can be selfishly motivated. However, our deepest need for approval comes from God and it is a good thing. When we speak of the people of God as "chosen people" we are talking about the way God Himself meets our deepest need to belong. He puts a feeling of emptiness inside us which only He can fill.

Psychologists affirm that the desire to belong is what makes loneliness so hard to bear. It is when we feel accepted and included that our self-esteem is satisfied. Pain comes from long periods of separation from loved ones and close friends with whom we feel a bond of affection. In the scriptures, God had something important to say about why He chose a people whom He could love and be loved by. That bond of affection between Himself and His people was totally undeserved.

God wants people who want Him. He chooses us first and then it is up to us to accept our being chosen. Knowing that in a real sense we do belong to Him is a satisfaction we find nowhere else.

This action of God which we endorse looks like a contract. But is not. It is a covenant. God will remain faithful to us even if we are not faithful to Him. A contract between two people is different. If there is a breach of a contract by either party, the other one can go to court for refunds of money paid out for work not done.

The difference here is that God never reneges on His promise to be faithful. Paul says:

"If we disown him, he will disown us. If we are faithless, he will remain faithful for he cannot disown himself." (2 Timothy 2:13)

We can happily conclude that God keeps because God cares. He could not care more.

Chapter 3

The Smile of God

"The Lord make His face shine upon you" (Numbers 6:25)

God has emotions just as we do. Often we express them without giving a thought to where they came from but only how to handle them. Our emotions are built in mechanisms for expressing what pleases or displeases us. Likewise, we learn in the Bible just how God feels about our desires and actions.

Let me list for you some of the chief feelings which the smile of God expresses:

He smiles at those who discover that He is infinitely more valuable than anything or anyone else. It is not that we are to treasure God somewhat but that we are to treasure Him most of all.

I think of the sad fact that the most qualified of Biblical students in Jesus' day were the Pharisees, but not one of them became a member of the team of disciples.

Jesus had ambivalent feelings about them. On the one hand, he must have applauded their devotion to the Scripture, although he never once said so. On the other hand, he was sternly critical of the way they made a project out of their faith and expected God to notice how good they were. They were great Biblical scholars, but they were also self-righteous hypocrites. They thought themselves to be worthier for being experts in all spiritual matters.

Their problem was their motivation. Jesus watched them show off their piety and he had only harsh words to say about them. We cannot build up a spiritual resume and expect favors from God for being "good." We cannot place God in our debt. We cannot make our faith into a tool.

T.S. Eliot wrote: "This above all is the greatest treason: to do the right thing for the wrong reason."[2] When we are self-righteous and expect God to reward us for it, we are saying that we do not want or need His undeserved favor and grace.

In the ancient world, the idea of using gods for human purposes was a common practice. Gods and goddesses were supposed to serve those who made sacrifices to them.

Edward Gibbon, in his classic "Fall of the Roman Empire" wrote: "The various modes of worship which prevailed in the Roman world were all considered by the people as equally true, by the philosophers as equally false, and by the magistrates as equally useful."[3]

If our religion is nothing more than a tool in the toolbox of our mind, we are sadly mistaken. If our faith is helpful in bolstering self-confidence, improving social stratus or being liked by certain people we want to impress, we will not have God's smile but only His frown.

God did give us the freedom to make choices and we should be happy that He did. God did not make robots, though I must confess, there were times when as a parent I wish He had. Robots always obey commands. But what satisfaction would come from hearing compliments from an electronic impulse? If my computer could talk, I am sure that it would tell me to go and get some basic computer science instruction. It would not give me any affection or encouragement.

My point is that God smiles when He knows that we freely choose to believe in Him and obey Him when we have the option to go our own way. Religion that is real and acceptable to God is not instrumental in the sense of being useful. It must be intrinsic and go deep into the personality where the soul and conscience reside. It is that place where the great exchange happens. In some miraculous and mysterious way, God takes our place on the cross. Vicariously, our sins are laid on Jesus and His righteousness is laid on us. It is the supreme expression of the mercy and grace of God, and the heart of the gospel good news.

God smiles when we are faithful to Him even when it is difficult and costly to do so. He is smiling when He sees us playing out our lives not to the crowd, not to impress anyone, because He knows that this leads to playing out our lives FOR the crowd. When we pray and say, "thine is the glory," we are making a promise that we are trying to live in such a way as to please Him.

It is something I call "spiritual physics." That is an analogy taken from the realm of natural law. I have a handmade Australian returning boomerang. I throw it a certain way into the sky, and it comes back to me. I think it is what Jesus had in mind when he was speaking of what we might call a reciprocal blessing.

"For with the measure you use it will be measured to you." (Luke 6:38)

We find the same principle operating in the marriage relationship. When I make my spouse happy, I am entering into that happiness myself. It is what the Psalmist had in mind when he wrote,

"Delight yourself in the Lord and He will give you the desires of your heart." (Psalm 37:1)

The Hebrew word for "delight" actually means "moldable, "or "malleable." If our desires are pliable enough to conform to what God desires for us, they can be molded like play dough into what we desire. That keeps us from making our faith into a tool to serve some purpose of our own. It is internalized where it becomes a way of enjoying the purposes for which God made us.

I think God smiles at us when we keep educating our conscience and keep it from being seared. The apostle Paul thought of it as a kind of quality control system which God built into all human beings. It is true that we can go against conscience and confuse what is good and right with what is not. Paul wrote that he was aware of this danger and said,

"I strive always to keep my conscience clear before God and man." (Acts 24:16)

If we do that, we will find that when we pray the Lord's prayer, we can say "thy kingdom come" while mentally we are thinking, "and my kingdom go!"

God also smiles when we realize that religion is not an academic subject to study but a relationship with Him to cultivate and maintain by our trust and obedience.

Suppose for a minute that you are in a college class entitled "The Bible as Literature" in the English department. It is opening day of class and the professor says to the students, "Now in this course we will not consider God as anyone more than a character in the Bible narrative."

This happened to the daughter of a friend of mine. When she told her father about that remark, the two of them agreed that she should drop the course. No one has the right to remake the Scriptures into a collection of stories whose heroes and heroines are simply role models for us to admire and emulate. While it is true that the Scriptures are literature they are much more. They are in a category by themselves as God's Word written.

It hurts our pride to be classified as a sinner needing to be rescued by a Savior. We might prefer to have someone be a cheerleader, a moral example who could inspire us to become a better self, or the ideal entrepreneur who achieves the American dream. The Bible never tells us how to take ourselves to the next level of our potential. Some think so and wish that the gospel were a kind of easy listening version of salvation by self-help. After all, doesn't the Bible say somewhere that "God helps those who help themselves?" No, it does not. The gospel is not advice; it is news of what God did for us that we could not do for ourselves. That is the gracious act of God we shall discuss in chapter 4.

Those people who think that God operates on a version of the merit system like the one used by the Scouts of America will always wonder how many badges of good works it takes to become good enough to earn God's favor. Perhaps, like me, they attended Sunday school as a child and were given a silver pin to wear with bars hanging down for perfect attendance for each year.

I remember that my motivation was all wrong. I was trying to get more silver bars than my friend David who was competing with me. You might say that what mattered was not learning about God but being in class each week. Unfortunately,it instilled within me the notion that God operates on a version of the merit system. That was something I had to unlearn the hard way and help others unlearn as well, counter cultural as it was.

People who are still thinking that way should probably not wear a cross but a small silver image of a weight scale. Such a scale is seen on the icon of justice, a woman holding a scale in her hand. Two pans are balancing each other. On the one pan there would be weights that stand for our sins, on the other pan there would be weights that stand for our good deeds. It is shown to weigh more than the other pan and thus signify that good deeds can compensate for our sin. This is a false assumption about the character of God.

The apostle Paul had to deal with the same misunderstanding in the church at Ephesus:

> "By grace you have been saved through faith, and this not from yourselves. It is the gift of God, not by works, so that no one can boast." (Ephesians 2:8,9)

God smiles when we are faithful and stand up for Him even when it is hard to do. He is happy when obedience to Him counts more than being popular and approved by other people. He is happy when we choose to play out our lives to an Audience of One, namely Himself. Knowing that this brings a broad smile to God's face is all the reward we could ever want.

Chapter 4

The Grace of God

"...and be gracious unto you" (Numbers 6:25)

The apostle Paul had the right attitude. He blamed his sinful nature on the law of sin operating within him even as he struggled to do what God wanted. The law of sin was waging war against the law of Paul's mind, making him its prisoner. Only a rescue from God would save him. Then he remembered that this is precisely what God had already done for him in Jesus Christ.

All of us have a public self, a private self and a secret self. It is in this third part of ourselves where we continually let God down and ourselves as well. We may be strong believers but the temptation to relax our guard is always present. We then do what we truly do not want to do. We need to be honest about this and come to God for the help only He can give. I refer to His grace and mercy.

Grace is God giving us the forgiveness we do not deserve. Mercy is God not giving us the punishment we do deserve. Lest we misunderstand this process, we need to make clear what grace is and what it is not. Yes, it really is amazing.

What grace does not mean

Grace does not mean making light of wrongdoing and overlooking it. It does not mean letting people walk all over us.

It does not mean pretending that nothing happened or denying what was said or done,

It does not mean putting someone on "probation" and saying, "Well, I forgive you this time, but it had better not happen again."

It does not mean that someone must admit being at least partly to blame.

It does not mean that we are not going to hold people accountable for their behavior.

What grace does mean

It does mean accepting an apology and offering to receive restitution of the value of what was broken or damaged by accident or carelessness.

It does mean doing our best not to let what happened spoil our friendship.

It does mean that we will not keep score of wrongdoing .

How God Forgives

As Christians, what we need to admit is that by our sin we have insulted God and rejected His rightful desire to control our lives. The famous author and evangelist of the last century, the late John Stott, said it best: "Man sins against God and puts himself where only God deserves to be; God sacrifices Himself for man and puts Himself where only man deserves to be."[4] This is the primary meaning of the cross and the supreme example of the gracious character of God.

God's mercy and grace work together in making possible what we call the "great exchange." In trusting in the grace of God and the death of Christ for our sins, we go to God and ask that He exchange our sins for Jesus' righteousness, and our disobedience for his perfect obedience. It takes true repentance to make this happen.

The problem has always been that many people take a very light view of sin. They have made Jesus into someone he never was. He is not the quintessential C.E.O. He is not going to help us experience everything we put into our "bucket list." He is not going to show us how we can tap into more of our potential and reach the American dream.

Repentance is not being remorseful and feeling sorry for having done something we regret. It is changing our mind and taking a different course of action.

Repentance is realizing that the subway train we are on is taking us in the wrong direction. It means getting off at the next stop, crossing over the tracks and then going down the stairs on the other side to wait for the train heading the opposite way. When it comes to practicing the Christian faith there seems to be a kind of upside-down but right-side up logic which takes some real getting used to.

There can be nothing harder for a Christian than to accept the requirement to set aside all desire of getting even with those who harm us. Forgiveness is a very high bar to reach when someone does us wrong and has not repented or asked to be forgiven.

Here is a dramatic and unforgettable illustration of applied Christianity. It is a true story.

Once there was a family of four which included an unmarried daughter in her late twenties. She still lived at home, and commuted daily a few miles to a government cancer research center near Washington, D.C.

She had a hobby of raising and showing purebred bulldogs. In attending dog shows, she became friends with a local man with the same interest in dogs. At first, they became business partners but as time went on the relationship became a romance. However, the man was unhappily married. To justify the affair, he said he would soon be free to date since he was expecting a divorce to take place shortly.

It became apparent, however, that this was only a line to keep the relationship going and looking legitimate. After a while the woman decided to date other men who were single, eligible bachelors. Her business partner became furiously jealous. In a letter to her he wrote, "If I can't have you, then no one will!" However, she did not sense the urgency of the threat and simply ignored it.

One cold wintry morning, snow had fallen during the night. She left early to go and feed the dogs at the kennel, but her car would not start. Her brother was outside shoveling snow from the driveway about 100 feet away. He went over to her and said: "Just let off the brake, hold down the clutch and let the car roll down the hill. When you get up enough speed let the clutch out with the gearshift in second and the engine will turn over and start. Let me get in and show you how." She thanked her brother but added that she knew just how to do what he suggested.

The brother returned to shoveling snow from the driveway. As he did, he looked up land saw her partner's car coming down from the top of the hill. The partner had been parked and watching for her to come out and get into the car. The brother finished his shoveling and went inside for breakfast with his mother and father. As it was a Saturday, their father was home.

Sometime later the doorbell rang. A uniformed police officer asked to come in. He had a serious look on his face. What could be wrong? Then came the worst news. The daughter was dead. Her business partner gave in to his intense feelings of jealousy and carried through with his threat on her life.

Then he made a getaway out of state but soon returned for an unknown reason. Some police officers spotted him and pulled him over. The officers approached him with caution but before they could make an arrest, he took out his pistol and killed himself.

Inside the house both parents and son comforted each other as they agonized with tears. Hearing of the outcome of the arrest, they were relieved to know they would not have to endure a court trial. The father was somehow able to pull himself together enough to say in a loud voice, "You know, we have to forgive him! If we do not, God will not forgive us! Remember what we say in the Lord's Prayer about asking for forgiveness "as we forgive those who trespass against us." Then they all hugged each other and cried.

How do I know this story is true? It is because I was the brother shoveling snow in the driveway that morning. I was home on the semester break from theological school. Writing about it has been hard, even though it was many years ago. However, God has healed the memory enough so that I can retell the story now without the sorrow and pain I once felt.

Sad as my story is, what could be sadder than the horrible murder of Jesus, the perfect and innocent Savior of the world? Jesus looked at those who were crucifying him with genuine forgiveness in his heart. and even said so as he spoke from the cross. How very true it was that the ones who wanted him dead really did not know what they were doing. When we think about the generosity of God's love that extends to the worst offenders, we must be amazed at His grace.

The Principle of Binding and Loosing

I am grateful to the late Catherine Marshall, wife of Peter Marshall, former Chaplain to the U.S. Senate, for her insight into this text from Matthew's gospel. Jesus said:

> "I tell you the truth, whatever you bind on earth will be bound in heaven, and whatever you loose on earth will be loosed in heaven." (Matthew18:18)

Catherine had been visiting with the Rev. David Duplessis, a South African Pentecostal minister, when she asked him about the meaning of the verse. " I was puzzled," she said, "until I learned that if I hang on to my judgment of another person and do not forgive, I am binding him to the very condition I would like to see changed. By unforgiveness I stand between the other person and the Holy Spirit's working in our relationship. By stepping out of the way and releasing someone from my judgment, I do not mean that the person is right, and I am wrong. No, what I mean is that they can be as wrong as they can be, but I will not be the judge."[5]

This is the prayer of relinquishment in which we say that we truly want God's will more than our own. We do not know enough to make an accurate judgment. Only He understands.

> "Therefore, if you are offering your gift at the altar and there remember that your brother has something against you, leave your gift there in front of the altar. First, go and be reconciled to your brother, then come and offer your gift." (Matthew 5:23,24)

I recall a member of my parish in Houston, now deceased, who had a unique understanding of forgiveness. If ever someone would do her wrong or act selfishly, she would think to herself, "Obviously, I don't know this person very well. There must be a hidden side to her which, if I understood it, would cause me to want to be her friend. So, I will just keep on believing and looking for that hidden side. I will relinquish my presumptions until I learn more and know her better." She says it turned her from being a prosecutor into being a defense attorney. It restored the relationship between them.

Dying versus Perishing

"God so loved the world that He gave His only Son that whosoever believes in Him should not perish but have everlasting life." (John 3:16)

Does the word "perish" seem out of place? Dying is natural and will happen to everyone, believer and unbeliever alike. Perishing is another thing altogether. It is the opposite of eternal life. It is not the life-giving presence of God forever but His absence forever. Jesus used the real-life example of an atrocity and an accident to illustrate the truth that there is no one who does not need to repent for sins:

"Now there were some present at that time who told Jesus about the Galileans whose blood Pilate had mixed with their sacrifices. Jesus answered, "Do you think that these Galileans were worse sinners than all the other Galileans because they suffered this way? I tell you no, but unless you repent, you will all perish. Or those eighteen who died when the tower in Siloam fell on them...do you think they were more guilty than all the others living in Jerusalem? I tell you no! But unless you repent, you too will all perish." (Luke 13:1-5)

Pilate had a problem with keeping order and preventing violence. Word of riots had gotten back to the Emperor and one more such report would likely end the governor's career. The question was this: Were those people killed that day worse sinners than all the other Galileans in the crowd?

What Jesus wanted the disciples to understand from his two examples is that no one is without sin. Everyone has flaws of character and thus everyone has a need to confess their sins. The famous promise of Jesus in John 3:16 has a condition which limits the promise only to believers.

They will die but not perish. Their souls live on forever in the perfect life in heaven.

The Thorn in the Flesh.

> "To keep me from becoming conceited because of these surpassing great revelations, there was given me a thorn in my flesh, a messenger of Satan to torment me. Three times I pleaded with the Lord to take it away from me. But he said to me, "My grace is sufficient for you, for my power is made perfect in weakness." Therefore, I will boast more gladly about my weaknesses, so that Christ's power may rest on me." (2 Corinthians 12:7-10)

This is a most interesting metaphor. First, Paul says that something in the flesh is troubling him. While never identifying just what it was, he does tell us that God had given it to him. He calls it a "thorn in the flesh."

Secondly, he says that God used Satan as a messenger to bring it to him.

Thirdly, he says that God gave it to him to keep him from the pride of having "great revelations" and to prevent his boasting about how "spiritual" he was.

No doubt that Paul had been having several special revelations from God and while it may have been enjoyable to Paul, God saw the danger of pride and gave him the solution. It was a painful "thorn" in his body. Curiously, he said that Satan delivered it. This shows that Satan is clearly under God's authority.

God's grace is always enough

Paul prayed to the Lord three times to remove this thorn. We wonder if "three" times simply meant many times. Paul waited and listened, and God finally said to him that he was not going to remove the thorn. Paul needed to depend more on God, not less. That called for endurance of the thorn, not its removal. Then God went on to explain that He was answering Paul's prayer but in a different but "sufficient" way. Paradoxically, healing would come by leaving the thorn unhealed. The Greek word for "sufficient" means that the supply is in exact proportion to the need. While that may well be true, we still stumble over the apparent contradiction in God's methodology of healing. He seems to be saying that He heals by not healing. This is another paradox we need to probe further for hidden meaning.

A few years ago, I made a study of the paradoxes we find in the teaching of Jesus. I mentioned that a paradox is a word picture that takes two seemingly opposite things and holds them together in tension until a new truth emerges.

Now let's consider how weakness could possibly be strength.

First, what is weakness? The late author and theologian J. I. Packer wrote that "weakness is a state of inadequacy in relation to some standard or ideal to which we desire to conform."[6]

The thorn may well refer to all the physical violence Paul endured (2 Corinthians 11:23-27) or perhaps an eye disease (2 Corinthians 4:15) or some other physical problem.

Personally, I believe it is good that Paul did not spell it out. I say that because the identity of the thorn is not necessary for us to know. It is best to leave it as some kind of affliction that won't go away, but which was nonetheless purposeful, It was sent from God and delivered by Satan and the purpose was to "harass" Paul, to humble him and keep him from making too much of his heavenly visions.

Let's stop right here to remind ourselves that human pride is the chief sin. If God gives us something to humble us and keep us prayerfully dependent on Him, then we are receiving a gift.

However. the thorn manifested itself in Paul, it can take various shapes in us. It can be painful to bear, but which we need to see as discipline. Oddly, we realize at some point that we are better people and better disciples of Jesus because we are operating under His control and not our own. The more we delve into this and other paradoxes, the more we can identify with Paul and say:

"Therefore, I will boast more gladly about my weaknesses
so that Christ's power may rest on me.

That is why, for Christ's sake, I delight in weaknesses, insults, hardship, in persecutions, in difficulties.

For when I am weak, then I am strong". (2 Corinthians 12:10)

In another passage, Paul put it this way:

> "I am crucified with Christ, and I no longer live but Christ lives in me. The life I live in the body, I live by faith in the Son of God, who loved me and gave himself for me." (Galatians 2:20)

God was leading Paul to the place where he could pray and honestly say that he wanted God more than he wanted answers. If answers were given too quickly, God could become in his mind something akin to a spiritual vending machine.

God hears all our prayers including the ones He seems not to answer. No prayer is wasted.

What this means is that we must relinquish the prayer for what we want and pray instead for what God wants for us. Give God the right to say no if He chooses to do so. Meanwhile, remember that He sees around corners, and sees the end from the beginning.

If you and I knew everything He knows, there would be many prayers we would like to take back.

Only with that caveat would St.Paul dare to say,

> "I can do everything through him who gives me strength." (Philippians 4:13)

There is a huge difference between asking the Lord to remove the thorn and asking for strength to allow the thorn to stay in place. We pray as we should by asking God to filter our prayers through the sieve of His will.

The problem of unanswered prayer

Another insight from the story of the thorn is that God will sometimes give us a different answer which is best for us but hard to recognize. Why does God do this? What could be better for Paul to succeed in his ministry than for God to take away the pain of the "thorn?" We don't know. But God does know and does not tell us what it is.

Author and pastor Timothy Keller explains that God will grant us only what is best for us. "When you struggle in prayer you can come before God with the confidence that He is going to give you what you would have asked for if you only knew everything He knows."[7]

In the following story, my wife, Dawn, writes how disciplining her children can be painful to them but that sometimes it is best to give them loving punishment. [8]

(Dawn Lawrence writing) " When I was three or four years old, I lived on Main Street in the small Pennsylvania town of Manheim. We did not have a backyard and so I was permitted to play out front if I did not go up the driveway past the crack in the sidewalk, which led to the road.

Our physician lived two doors down and he had a son, Joey. We often played together. One day we were riding our broomstick horses and he said, "My uncle has a real horse. Would you like to go and see it?" I said "yes", and we headed up busy Main Street. His uncle lived outside of town, and on the way, we had to cross several intersections.

When Dr. Weaver and my mother discovered that we were missing, they headed out to search for us. Shortly they found us riding our broomsticks up the busy street. Dr. Weaver said to Mother, "You know what we are going to have to do." Mother nodded in agreement.

And so, arriving back home, Mother took me over her knee and spanked me and then placed me in my crib. I will never forget that day I met Joey at our fiftieth high school reunion a few years ago. He came over and asked, "Do you remember the time when......." Smiling, we both remembered being paddled. Looking back, I am thankful to God for a mother who loved me enough to discipline me when I needed it.

We are shocked when we hear the application to by Jesus.

> "So shall my Heavenly Father do to each of you if you do not forgive your brother from your heart." (Matthew 18:35)

Notice the word "heart." We are to bury the hatchet of our desire to payback the wrongdoing. Instead, we must forget where we buried it. So much is said by that two-letter word in the Lord's prayer, the word 'as." We are to copy the way God forgives and keep it in our minds as a model.

Is there a line drawn somewhere to separate wrongs we must forgive and those we can ignore? No, there is no such line. Jesus was dying on the cross with forgiveness on his lips for those who put him there. If Jesus could do that, we have no excuse for doing any less. If we won't forgive others, then neither will God forgive us. It is the one thing God won't do.

Chapter 5

The Attention of God

"In short, God will either give us what we ask for or what we would have asked for if we knew everything He knew."
Tim Keller

When we welcome what someone has to say to us, we turn our face toward him or her and pay full attention. Sometimes when we do not want to hear, we turn our face away, perhaps with a phony excuse. Body language will communicate our real feelings.

Facial expressions can tell us so much without our saying one word. Smiles and frowns have power to demonstrate our moods, whether we want to talk about some issue, whether we want to share our feelings, or whether we want to give our undivided attention. Turning our face toward someone means recognizing their presence and showing pleasure. Turning our face away from someone is a strong clue to our displeasure.

It was King Hezekiah, a good and godly man of God, who sent a proclamation to be read aloud by couriers as they went from town to town. The king gave the proclamation as a way of reminding the people not to neglect the celebration of Passover. By so doing, they would have an opportunity to rededicate themselves to the Lord as they praised Him for all their blessings.

King Hezekiah wrote:

"The Lord your God is gracious and compassionate. He
will not turn his face from you if you return to him."
(2 Chronicles 30:9)

"Countenance" in Hebrew is the same word as "face." King David
used the word as he prayed:

"Let the light of your face shine upon us, O God."
(Psalm 4:6)

In this time of insecurity resulting from the Covid 19 pandemic, it
helps to remember how in the Bible, God asked His people to trust that
He knows all about their problems. While we work on human solutions
to our pandemic and invent vaccinations to protect the spread of the virus,
He does not want us to trust Him any less. It is perfectly all right with
Him to leave us wondering how the answer will come, and what it will be.
Meanwhile, we are to leave the matter in His hands.

I am reminded of the line in the Old Testament where a king named
Jehoshaphat was threatened by an army of enemy soldiers with tremendous
military power. He prayed to God and said words you and I could just as
well pray in our time.

"O God, we have no power to face this vast army that is
attacking us. We do not know what to do but our eyes are
upon you." (2 Chronicles 20:12)

My point is that we are not informing God of anything He does not
know. We are saying that we know that He is still in charge of the universe,
which He made, and that we can trust that He will see us through our
troubles. If we can trust in a man-made electronic marvel like the Global
Positioning System in our car to show us how to get to our destination, we
can certainly trust God for much more.

We would do well to think of the message of an ad for an airline, which
was on a roadside billboard. The sign showed the picture and brand name
of the airline and underneath the picture in large letters was this clever
message, "YOUR OTHER GPS." We can say that and more about God
in His role of guiding us in difficult times like these.

Whose battle is it?

We often forget that throughout the Bible God portrays our struggle with forces that oppose Him as a battle. Evil is shown to be the work of Satan and his opposition to everything right and good and just. God is contending with the pagan gods of the culture and peoples already in the land. God knew that settling His people into the land of promise would require a full-scale attack on both human and spiritual enemies.

However, the people of God assumed that the outcome of the battles was their responsibility. They might need to call for help but they thought that winning or losing was entirely up to them.

The truth is just the opposite. God is not our cheerleader waiting for us to win battles for Him. No, it is not that we are fighting for God with help as needed from Him. Rather it is God who is fighting for us, not we for Him. He does not expect us to be winning battles for Him and then to be proudly displaying what great soldiers we are. Our business is to unmask false gods which deceive people and lead them into idolatry and self-destructive behaviors.

There can be no gloating over any victory that results by confronting these gods. We are not trying to prove how strong we are but how strong He is. The victory is not ours but God's to win and claim.

The wording of the Lord's Prayer is a clue to this distinction. We ask God to deliver us from evil. That means a rescue. Our human pride wants to take at least some credit for success. However, would a lifeguard, hearing a cry for help, call to the person in trouble and shout, "You swim ten feet and I will come and get you there?" No, the battle is not mostly the Lord's, but entirely His.

Dreams can be so real. When I awaken from a bad one, I want to get up for fear the dream will continue. Who knows how it will end? I am not one to take real life risks lightly. Prudence means taking calculated risks when we must do so. Yet at the same time we use our common sense. We set aside funds for future needs. We buy life insurance. We put seat belts around our waists when we drive cars. Minimizing risk is simply the smart thing to do.

Nevertheless, when dreams about "what if?" disrupt our sleep, we can respond by turning worst-case scenarios into best-case realities. In these days when we must fight an invisible enemy called Covid 19, we can comfort ourselves with the greatest dragon killer truth we could ever have: We live on this side of Easter.

Anyone who dies and does not stay dead has to be taken seriously for who He claims to be. The story of Easter is not fiction but fact. It is history, and the fact which made B.C. (Before Christ) into A.D. (Anno Dominus), meaning the "reign of the Lord." It is silent testimony of every calendar, of believer and unbeliever alike, that history began again with the coming of Christ. He is truly the "hinge" of history.

The woman who wore the ancient amulet with the blessing of God inscribed on tiny scrolls did not yet know about Easter. God did, but it was centuries into the future. What she did have was the evidence that a God who could lead His people out of Egypt and across the Red Sea was a God who had shown Himself to be worthy of her trust.

In the same way, we believe and trust in a promise- making, promise-keeping God. He has many ways of showing His worthiness to make "what if" become the "even if." God will never let us down.

The light of His countenance

Light was the first of things God created for this world. The light/darkness motif runs throughout the Bible, light standing for God, while darkness is standing for evil and the works of Satan. Light is a kind of generic word, which Scripture uses to refer to God's guidance. We see that guidance during the long march to the promised land. The people had the privilege of a moving cloud by day and a moving fire by night. It was their primitive but effective GPS. Here are some key Old Testament verses among many others which support this truth:

"In your light we see light" (Psalm 36:9)

"Send out your light and your truth, let them lead me" (Psalm 43:3)

"The Lord is my light and my salvation," (Psalm 27:1)

"When I sit in darkness, the Lord will be a light unto me." (Micah7:8)

The Holy Spirit is the guiding light we need when things are going well and when they are not. He does for us what light does to darkness. Jesus' claim to be the "light of the world" is one of His most profound of all. It would be the height of arrogance were it not literally as well as figuratively true. The promise which follows is of great comfort to all who trust in Him.

> "I am the light of the world. He who follows me will not walk in darkness but will have the light of life." (John 8:12)

It is worth noting that the phrase "lift up the light of his face" in the Bible always has a human subject. It refers to an act of turning and looking towards someone to convey a sense of acceptance and favor.

In my mind, I picture the appearance of a well-known politician in front of applauding audience of supporters. The politician sees a familiar face in the crowd and then, with a broad smile, extends a pointing finger to say, "Thank you."

It is also worth noting that this original Hebrew blessing reads with a sense of a crescendo building from the first line to the third and last line. It suggests that the blessings of guarding and protecting, showing mercy and grace, culminate in a grand purpose. That purpose is to live in and enjoy harmony and peace with God and other people. It announces that message as though it were the finale of a great musical composition.

Before we enter the last chapters of this book it is worth noting that many modern people see the Christian faith as something we learn to outgrow because it is immature, even naïve. That is wrong. The Christian mindset is something we have been learning about since our birth and it shapes our worldview as adults. Yes, even at the beginning of life God is preparing not just our bodies for birth but every other part of our being to know and love Him. Listen to how Isaiah speaks about this literal and figurative kind of "carrying" by God.

> "Listen to me, O house of Jacob, all you who remain in the house of Israel, you whom I have upheld since you were conceived, and have carried since your birth. Even to your old age and gray hairs I am he who will sustain you. I have

39

made you and will carry you. I will sustain you and I will rescue you." (Isaiah 46:3-5)

Notice how God says that He upholds us beginning with our conception. Here is Biblical evidence that God regards our conception as the beginning of our existence. There is a continuing debate about this in every generation.

It is an astounding claim which has not changed as human beings progress to new levels of knowledge in the medical and technological fields. We can never educate ourselves out of our dependence on God.

The bottom line is that God in one way or another is always lifting us. He lifts us out of our ignorance, out of our pride, our loneliness, into the mindset that He is in control, and always present with us.

Think for a minute about the small drones that are much more than toys. Realtors use them to take pictures of properties from 100 feet altitude. Likewise, God lifts us high above what our human eyes and minds perceive to the unseen and eternal world of the Spirit. Realtors have a bird's eye view of a property they are selling. In a similar way, God gives us the perspective of eternity on every ambition, every idea of success, every assumption of what makes for happiness.

What price do you put on God's view on such things from the perspective of eternity? You can't. But He delights in lifting you high enough to let you see it.

The radiant face of Moses

"When Moses came down from Mount Sinai with the two tablets of the Testimony in his hands, he was not aware that his face was radiant because he had spoken with the Lord. When Aaron and all the Israelites noticed they were afraid to come near him. But Moses called to them. "So, Aaron and all the leaders of the community came back to him and he spoke to them. They saw that his face was radiant."(Exodus 34:29-31, 35).

That is the kind of disciples Jesus calls us to be. He calls us to such a deep transformation of our inner being that we can't help but let it show.

He calls us to be people who have such a compelling love for the Lord that others want to be with us and learn what is the explanation for being attractively different. The people who allow Christ to change them from the inside out can explain it by saying that something supernatural happened to them. The fact is that they are reflecting in their own personality the light that Jesus was shining on them.

> "Let your light shine before men, that they may see your good works and praise your Father in heaven." (Matthew 5:16)

The spiritual darkness of our world needs people who reflect the light of Christ the way the moon reflects the light of the sun. You and I can be those people who will make our dark world a little brighter, safer and easier to live in as disciples of Christ.

Chapter 6

The Peace of God

"...and give you peace" (shalom) (Numbers 6: 27)

C hristmas time always points me to the words of the angel Gabriel announcing the birth of the Savior:

> "Glory to God in the highest and on earth peace on whom
> his favor rests." (Luke 2:14)

Did you note the condition? The Shalom (peace) of God comes to those with whom He is well pleased. If we cannot sing "O come let us adore Him" and mean it, if what we want is the gift of peace but not the peace Giver, we will have neither the gift nor the Giver.

The angels got it right, of course. They saw peace as an integral part of glorifying God in the highest. Peace and glory are two sides of the same coin. This simple verse from the apostle Paul says it so well:

> "May the God of hope fill you with all joy and peace in
> believing." (Romans 15:13)

Step One to enjoying the shalom of God is realizing that in thought, words and deeds we have offended Him and need forgiveness. That takes genuine humility, and the willingness to accept our need of God's grace. It is nothing less, nothing more and nothing else.

This is the bold claim of the first commandment. If we allow anything or anyone, our career, our possessions, our friends, even our loved ones to be in first place we have an idol. That is why we sing at Christmas time, "O come let us adore him, Christ the Lord." We do not sing "come let us admire him," or "come let us respect him," but "come let us adore (worship) him."

In the original Hebrew, shalom was used to refer to physical and material wellbeing. For example, in Genesis Jacob asks Joseph, his son, to go and check on the shalom of his brothers and of the cattle.

Shalom also extends into the realm of social relationships. People are often without shalom when injustice and oppression go unchecked. The presence of positive and just social relationships is the earmark of things being as God wants them.

We also find the word being used to designate morality and integrity. Shalom refers to the opposite of shame, guilt, deceit and hypocrisy. It means working to promote honesty and fairness at all levels. Where true shalom is, things are the way God intended for them to be. When people aim at wanting to know and do God's will, shalom results.

In the New Testament shalom carries forward some of the same core meanings as the Hebrew shalom. Peace in the New Testament is also linked with the Holy Spirit as a fruit of His work in our lives as believers.

This list of these fruit is found in Paul's letter to the church in Galatia.

> "The fruit of the Spirit is love, joy, peace, patience, kindness, goodness, faithfulness, gentleness and self-control." (Galatians 5:22)

One thing shalom does not mean

Some may expect that shalom was the Old Testament way of speaking about what we know as pacifism. The truth is that the Old Testament does not know about this concept. Nor does it show us any examples of it in the lives of its characters. There is no mention of the subject of disarmament to achieve a peaceful relationship between nations. These are legitimate questions to raise about war and peace, but they are not brought up as meanings of shalom.

What we can learn from this is that the use of a word is the most reliable key to its meaning. What we find in this word is many meanings like the New Testament word "gospel," but without any mention of salvation from sin.

The New Testament, building as it does on the continuing narrative of the first or Old Testament, adds new meaning to shalom without detracting anything from the Old Testament concept. That new meaning has to do with the coming of Christ as Messiah to bring to the world salvation from our sin. The concept of sin was not included in the multiple meanings of shalom.

What we must not miss is the honesty with which the New Testament writers speak about their own need for a Savior. Paul himself owned up to the fact that he had persecuted Christians before his conversion and because of that he regarded him as the worst of all candidates to be a leader and apostle. This illustrates the wideness of God's mercy.

The apostle Paul lists for his readers the kinds of people who will not inherit the kingdom of God, except by God's grace.

> "Do you not know that the wicked will not inherit the kingdom of God? Do not be deceived: Neither the sexually immoral nor adulterers nor male prostitutes nor homosexual offenders nor thieves nor the greedy nor drunkards nor slanderers nor swindlers will inherit the kingdom of God. That is what some of you were. But you were washed. You were sanctified in the name of the Lord Jesus Christ and by the Spirit of our God." (1 Corinthians 6:11)

Those are strong words. They tell us that everyone needs a Savior! This includes all those who were called by Jesus as his disciples and all who worked alongside the apostle Paul in his wide -reaching ministry to the ancient world. All the followers of Jesus are saved by grace alone, through Christ alone, through faith alone, but not by a faith that is alone. In both Old and New Testaments, peace is the product of God's grace and that grace comes by the cross of Christ. There is no one who is exempt from the need of grace, and no one who finds the peace of God without it.

The Paradox of the Peaceful Sword

In the gospel of Matthew, we read that Jesus said:

> "Do not suppose that I have come to bring peace to
> the earth. I did not come to bring peace but a sword."
> (Matthew 10:34)

It sounds as though Jesus was contradicting himself. Did not Isaiah the prophet say that Messiah would come as the prince of peace? Did not Jesus himself ask his followers to be peacemakers? Yes. Remember that in both Testaments we learn that there is a battle going on between the forces of good and evil. We should not be surprised that the metaphor of a sword might symbolize our fighting against unseen spiritual enemies commanded by Satan himself.

For example, in the book of Hebrews we read:

> "God's word is like a sharp, two-edged sword, living
> and active, judging thoughts and attitudes of the heart."
> (Hebrews 4:12)

It is one of the various pieces of spiritual armor for believers to use to stand against evil.

> "Put on the full armor of God so that you can take your
> stand against the devil's schemes" (Ephesians 6:11)

Comparing the armor of a Roman soldier to a battle-ready Christian, Paul says that the sword of the Spirit is the "Word of God," or as we sometimes put it, "God's Word written." We mean the Bible.

A demonstration of the truth of this metaphor occurs in the story of the temptation of Christ by Satan as recorded in Matthew 4. Each time Satan presented a temptation, Jesus simply quoted a pertinent verse of Scripture. Satan did not argue with Jesus but simply changed the temptation. What that means is that there is in the Scripture an inherent authority, which must be recognized as being the last word. It is encouraging for all of us to remember that when we find ourselves in a spiritual battle, we can take a stand just as Jesus did and know that the Scripture cannot be overturned. It is like our Supreme Court with authority above all other authorities. Satan is defeated as we stand our ground on its truth. We also note that a sword has room in its handle for only one hand. If your hand is in that handle no one else's hand is there with yours. We cannot fight on the grounds of anyone else's faith but our own.

The peace of God is a powerful witness

Julie, a member of my parish in Houston, suffered serious injuries from an auto accident when she was 23 years old. It was a one-car accident that broke her neck. She lost control of her vehicle and, unfortunately, she was not wearing a seat belt. She is called a quadriplegic because she is totally paralyzed in both of her legs and arms.

She was taken to a Houston hospital by helicopter and to a specialist who saved her life. When she recovered enough to speak her attitude was amazingly positive. She believed that eventually she would walk again. Soon she learned that she would always be confined to her wheelchair.

Nonetheless, she turned to her strong commitment to Christ and found peace in accepting her condition. "For every problem there is a solution," her mother had taught her. Julie thought, "Yes, I recall a verse in the Bible where it says,

'I can do everything through him who gives me strength" (Philippians 4:13)

"Looking back over the years since," Julie said, "I saw God's hand in how He provided people who supported me in so many ways."

Over the years, Julie has coped very well with living as a quadriplegic and with all the restrictions that come with such a very serious disability. Despite it all, her life continues to be happy and fulfilling. She enrolled in a community college and learned how to become a paralegal. She never became cynical nor did she wrestle with such questions as "Why did this happen to me?"

Julie credits her strong trust in God to her mother who was always reminding her that God is with her in whatever life brings. Julie says, "God is the one who gave me the faith to go on and find true peace no matter what comes my way. I really feel humbled by it all."

I mentioned to her that she has a unique opportunity few others have. Living in a wheelchair with an attitude like hers is a silent and visible sermon, a testimony without any words. Her smiling face speaks loudly and makes for a powerful witness to the reality of the true shalom of God which comes as a gift from Christ.

"I believe," she said, "that I am a silent witness. People look at me in my wheelchair and wonder how I can smile as I tell my story. They notice my attitude and learn that I have allowed God to use me to show how I cope with tragedy as a Christian. This faith is what helps me live a life of happiness and not sorrow. I have not blamed anybody but myself for what happened. I just hope they see Christ in me."

She is a most attractive witness to how faith in Christ really works. In the past Julie has been a speaker at schools where she told her story and answered questions. She has also worked with Texas Institute for Rehabilitation in their speaking programs.

Julie is always smiling and ready to answer anyone who asks, "What happened?" She mentioned to me that people who wonder what to say to a severely handicapped person might say politely, "I don't want to offend you by my offer to help, but if there is something I can do for you, please let me know."[9]

We may not know why God allows heartbreak, but the answer must be important since He allowed His own heart to break at the cross. The cross is a powerful expression of God's grace and the ultimate demonstration of His love. That love is the source of our true shalom.

Sometimes I feel that one of the chief roadblocks to growth in our faith is false assumptions and sentimentalized expectations of what the Christian life entails. Jesus did not promise us a rose garden, but he did promise us a victory garden. By that I mean that troubles will come our way, but by God's grace, as we depend on Him, we will overcome them all.

Chapter 7

The Ownership of God

*"So, they will put my name on the Israelites,
and I will bless them" (Numbers 6:27)*

One of my favorite chapel talks I used to share with the boys and girls of our parish day school was the interactive talk on the ownership of God.

I would begin by asking the children to name one thing that God did not make. Someone might mention the church building. I pointed out that the church building is all brick, and bricks were made of clay which comes from the ground, which God owns. Another might mention an automobile. I showed them that everything a car is made from comes from raw materials in the ground. Steel comes from iron which is mined from the ground. Plastic comes from petroleum which comes from the ground. Likewise, glass comes from the sand taken from the ground. God owns the ground. Scripture reminds us of that:

"The earth is the Lord's and everything in it, the world
and all who live in it." (Psalm 24:1)

Several years ago, when buying a new car, I toyed with the salesman in the effort to help him understand this truth. He was drawing up the official bill of sale from the dealership to me. This was to provide me with legal proof of ownership until the day came when I traded it in for another car or sold it to a private party. He thought he was giving me a title deed. In the legal sense He was right. In a deeper sense, he was not.

I signed the papers. But God, of course, did not. All I had was some papers to give me the right to use the vehicle and consider it my property. The vehicle was nothing but a collection of materials taken from the ground and assembled in a factory into a car. Eventually, when it is worn out and no longer usable, it will be taken to an automobile graveyard. There it will rust and decay, eventually returning to the earth from which the raw materials came.

Not only is everything borrowed from God, but we ourselves are His property. The psalmist said it well:

> "You (God) knit me together in my mother's womb. I praise
> you for I am fearfully and wonderfully made; your works
> are wonderful; I know that full well." (Psalm 139:14)

Notice the passive voice. Human beings do not make themselves; they are made by the Maker, Almighty God. Only He gives life. Everything and everyone comes from God.

In addition to this we read in various parts of the Bible that while all human beings were His creation in the generic sense, there was from the beginning a called-out people. These would belong to Him in a special way through what was called a covenant. No less than five times God and His people promised in a solemn covenant to belong to each other. First it was with Noah, then Abraham, Moses, David and finally the New Covenant with Jesus Christ.

Occasionally God would remind His people of His covenant relationship with them. Here is a clear example:

> "Fear not, for I have redeemed you. I have summoned you
> by name. You are mine. You are precious and honored in
> my sight and I love you." (Isaiah 43:1,4)

During Israel's history God also chose to name a city, Jerusalem, as His own. It is the city which became known as the "city of God." He said,

> "In Jerusalem I will put my name. (2 Kings 21:4)

God also put His name on a building, the Temple in Jerusalem, built by David's son Solomon. Unfortunately, an enemy invasion destroyed it. A second temple which was less magnificent took its place. However, in the year 70 A.D. a rebellion of the people against the Romans led once again to its destruction.

In this series of covenants between God and His people the final and greatest covenant of all came about with the birth of Jesus. It was such a significant reset of history that the calendar literally began again. The part before the New Covenant was B.C. (Before Christ), and the part following the birth of Christ became the present age we know as A. D. (Anno Dominium), "in the year of the Lord's reign."

Many centuries of Christian history passed and in the early sixteenth century a bold German monk named Martin Luther became the first to reveal the need for a reformation of Christian doctrine. Before long other groupings of Christians joined in this wide movement of reform. Each group felt it necessary to have their own officially approved summary documents of what they believed.

Anglicans had their thirty-nine Articles of 1562, Presbyterians had their Westminster Confession of 1648, Lutherans had their Augsburg Confession of 1562. Churches tracing their beliefs to the broader Protestant Reformation had their own uniqueness and identity.

Churches grouping themselves in the various Christian Reformed traditions drafted the Heidelberg Confession. It was published in 1653 in question and answer form and designed to be memorized.

It begins with the question "What is your only comfort in life and death?"

Answer: "That I am not my own, but belong with my body and soul, both in life and death to my faithful Savior Jesus Christ. He as fully paid for all my sin by his precious blood and has set me free from the power of the devil. Jesus assures me of eternal life and makes me heartily willing to live from now on as his follower and disciple."[10]

Stop and ponder the meaning of not being our own. We do not belong to ourselves. Our identity is not about who we are but Whose we are. This does not mean that we are free to do what we please, but only that which honors God and pleases Him. We are to show that we belong to Him as we honor and follow our Savior, Jesus Christ.

Our business is to make Christ look as good and valuable and attractive and magnetically appealing as He really is. In fact, we can go so far as to say that when we say "Our Father" we are to think of the character of God as being like the ideal human father but without the flaws which even the best of fathers have.

Jesus shows us how to be the kind of disciples he wants us to be. A church in Houston has a kind of motto engraved in the concrete on the wall near the entrance. The sign reads:

"A disciple is one who loves Jesus, learns from him, follows him, and leads others to do the same."[11]

What we need in order to do this is a kind of deep humility. That should stir up within us gratitude for our generous God and His undeserved and uncontainable love.

Let us rely completely on the blessing of the Lord and remember what we have learned together in this book.

But let us rely even more on the Lord of the blessing. We don't just have the Word of God, the Bible, precious as it is. We have Jesus the Savior who did everything needed for us to be put right with God. We know that we are His and He is ours forever. How do we put a value on that? We don't. We simply rejoice that God is the generous God He is. That is what makes Him smile, and makes us feel truly content.

Chapter 8

Questions for discussion or reflection

Chapter 1

1. What definition of blessing means the most to you?
2. Why is there nothing we can do to make God love us more or love us less?
3. What does it mean to say that grace comes before the law, not after?
4. Why must people know they are spiritually lost before they can be found?

Chapter 2

1. What would you have said to the orderly in the hospital?
2. Why does keeping include dying?
3. What is the difference between mercy and grace?
4. What does it mean to "perish"?

Chapter 3

1. What is it that keeps us from making God our supreme treasure?
2. What reason did God have in mind for giving human beings the freedom to choose their way or His way?
3. What is meant by "spiritual physics?"
4. How do we know what God delights in?
5. What kept Jesus from choosing disciples from the Bible scholars known as Pharisees?
6. Which reasons for God's smile of approval sounds most credible to you?

Chapter 4

1. What is the difference between remorse and regret versus real repentance?
2. What was the biggest obstacle for Jews to accept Jesus as their Messiah?
3. What is the prayer of relinquishment?
4. What is the one thing God will not do?

Chapter 5

1. How is God like a spiritual GPS?
2. Why is our battle really God's battle?
3. What comfort is there in knowing that we live on this side of the empty tomb of Jesus?
4. In practical terms, how do we "keep an eye on God (Jesus)?"

Chapter 6

1. For you what is the most meaningful definition of "shalom?"
2. What does the "sword" of Jesus mean?
3. In your mind what is the difference between peace as the world gives and peace that Jesus gives?
4. How is this peace beyond our understanding?

Chapter 7

1. Why is belonging such a strong psychological need?
2. Name four places where God has put His name.
3. In this American culture why is it hard to accept the truth of the Heidelberg Catechism: "You are not your own?" Consider Paul's words where he writes, "you were bought with a price." (I Corinthians 6:20)

End Notes

1 Episcopal Church, *The Book of Common Prayer*, (New York, Seabury Press, 1979) p. 331

2 Eliot, T. S. *Murder in the Cathedral*, (New York, Faber and Faber, 1938)

3 Gibbon, Edward, *Decline and Fall of the Roman Empire* (New York, Harcourt Brace, 1960)

4 Stott, John, *The Cross of Christ*, (Leicester, England, Intervarsity Press, 1986) p. 60

5 Marshall, Catherine, *Something More*, (Carmel, New York, Guideposts Associates, 1974) p.38

6 Packer, J. I., *Weakness is the Way*, (Wheaton, Il. Crossway Publishers, 2013) p, 49

7 Keller, Tim, *Prayer*, (New York: Penguin Press, 2014) p.228

8 Lawrence, Dawn, written at the author's request and given by her permission

9 Julie's story, requested by the author and given by Julie's permission

10 Heidelberg Catechism, www.gotquestions.org/Heidelberg-Catechism html last updated 4/20/2021

11 A sign with words set in concrete, Tallowood Baptist Church, Houston, Tx